Mary Cohen

Superduets 2

Fantastic cello duets
for the well-established beginner

© 1998 by Faber Music Ltd
First published in 1998 by Faber Music Ltd
This edition published in 2001 by Faber Music Ltd
3 Queen Square London WC1N 3AU
Cover illustration by Todd O'Neill
Music processed by Mary Cohen and Jeanne Fisher
Printed in England by Caligraving Ltd
All rights reserved

ISBN 0-571-51892-3

To buy Faber Music publications or to find out about the full range of titles available
please contact your local music retailer or Faber Music sales enquiries:

Faber Music Limited, Burnt Mill, Elizabeth Way, Harlow, CM20 2HX England
Tel: +44 (0)1279 82 89 82   Fax: +44 (0)1279 82 89 83
sales@fabermusic.com   www.fabermusic.com

Contents

To the teacher

Superduets 2 for cello is designed for well-established beginners who can play the one-octave scales and arpeggios of D and G major and have a repertoire of pieces using Finger Pattern One (placing the semitone between the third and fourth fingers). It can be used as the sequel to *Superduets 1* or with any other standard material.

Duets are a wonderful introduction to social music making and this tuneful collection contains a wide variety of styles and many different string techniques. Each piece has helpful rehearsal and performance tips to encourage pupils to think, listen and count. All the pieces in this book are compatible with *Superduets 2* for violin. By the end of the book pupils should be ready to tackle beginner string quartets [†].

Mary Cohen

[†] for example, *Quartetstart* (available from Faber Music)

Professor Peg-Box

listens to the woodpeckers at the bottom of his garden

FACT FILE: col legno — bounce the wood of the bow gently against the strings.
REHEARSAL TIP: Work at the 'improvisation' bars (D to E) several times by themselves until they always fit into the music without spoiling its flow.

Moderato

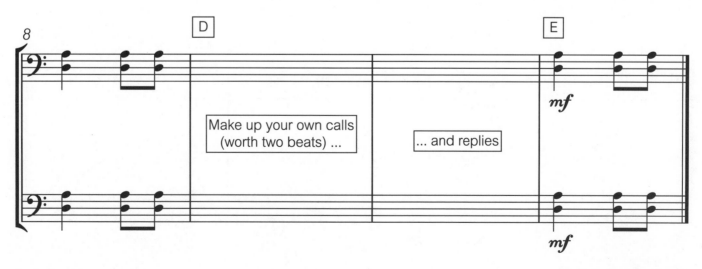

Make up your own calls (worth two beats) ...

... and replies

Signor Pizzicato

dances the polka

BRAIN TEASERS: Where do both parts play pizzicato? Bar ....
Which part has the tune and which has the accompaniment?
REHEARSAL TIP: If your part has the tune, play it out; if your
part has the accompaniment, listen to the tune as you play.

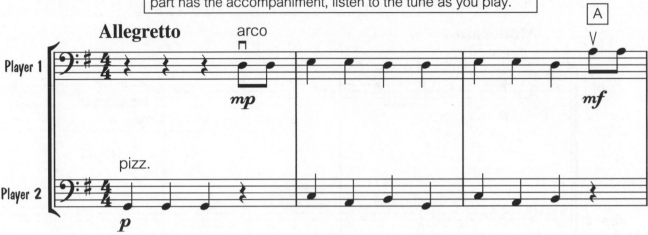

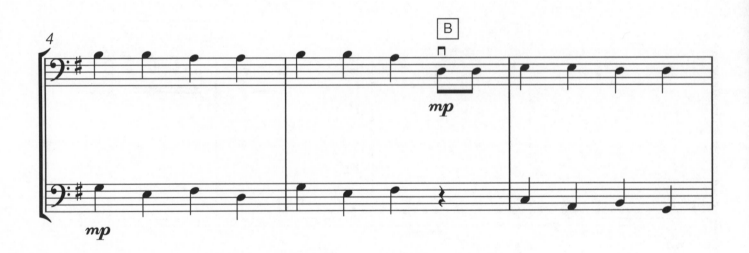

Major Marvel

goes skating and hums a half-remembered tune

CHALLENGE: Play the accented notes > with extra energy
(these are the places where Major Marvel falls over!).
BRAIN TEASER: Which tune is Major Marvel half-remembering?

Gabriella's Octopus

is always very friendly
(watch out — he likes shaking hands with everyone at once)

BRAIN TEASER: Where does Gabriella's Octopus shake hands with himself to make an octave? Bars .... , ... , ... and .... .

Mrs Andantino

goes for a walk

BRAIN TEASER: What does 'Da Capo al Fine' mean?

Mister Misterioso

tells a story

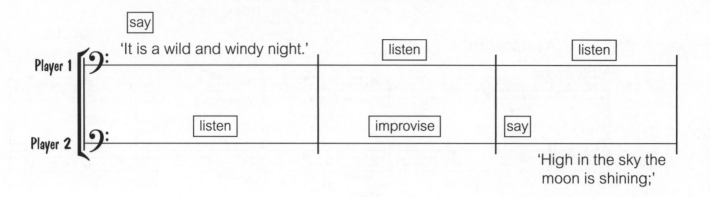

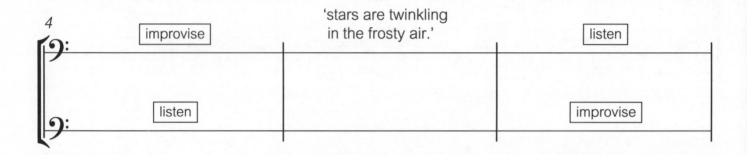

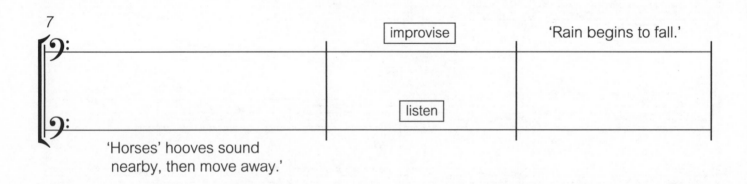

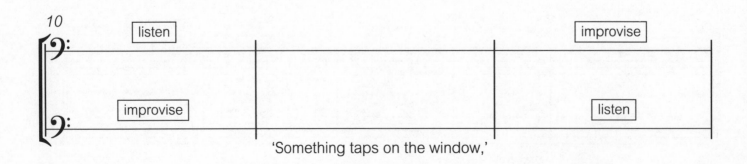

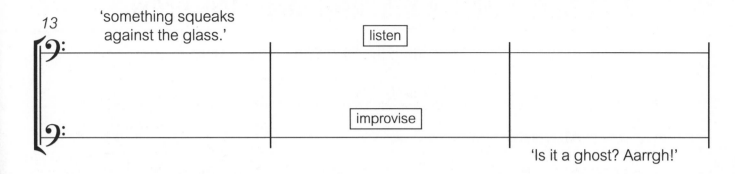

'Is it a ghost? Aarrgh!'

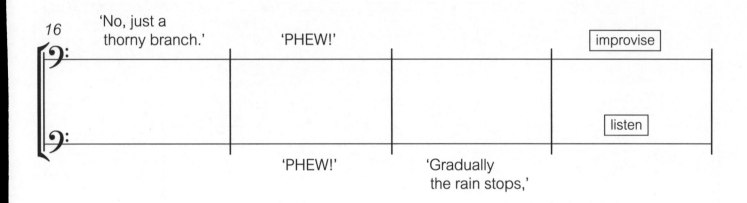

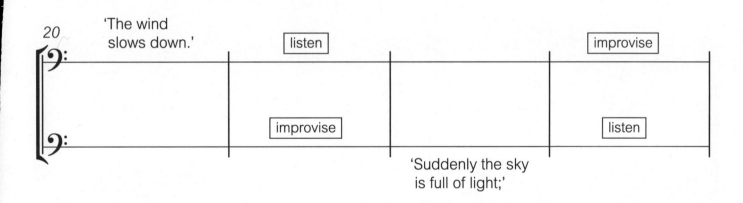

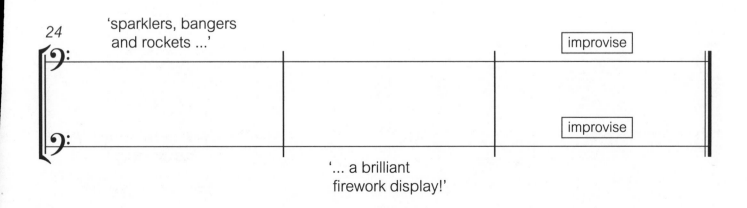

Captain Fortissimo and his fire crew

get hot and bothered

BRAIN TEASER: How many times does
each fireman climb up and down a ladder?

second time fade away

second time fade away

General Pause
stops to think

CHALLENGE: In all the 'GP' bars imagine
the sound of the music you have just played.

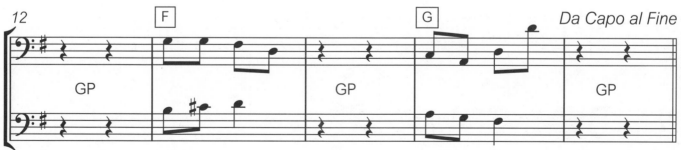

Doctor Canon

tries to catch up

BRAIN TEASER: Does he ever manage to catch up?

Mister Misterioso
floats away

TECHNICAL TIP: Play these harmonics half-way along the string which has the same letter name as the printed note; touch the string lightly with the pad of your little finger, and use long bows. FACT FILE: sul tasto — play lightly over or near the fingerboard.

Signorina Ritardando

slows down at the end of a busy day

BRAIN TEASER: Which Italian word means 'slow down'? REHEARSAL TIP: The player whose part has the most 'moving' notes should lead the slowing down.

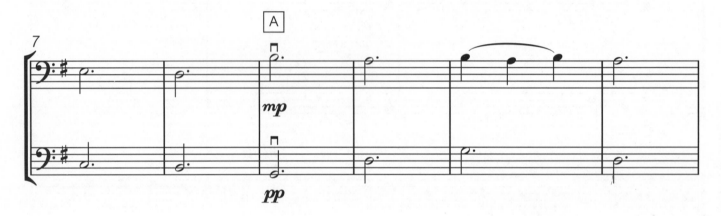

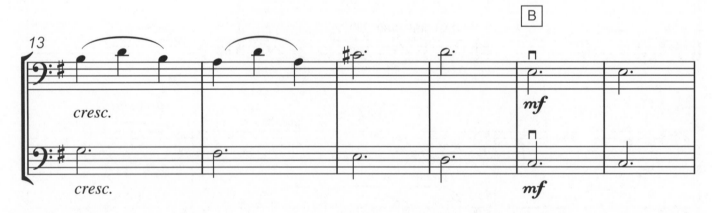

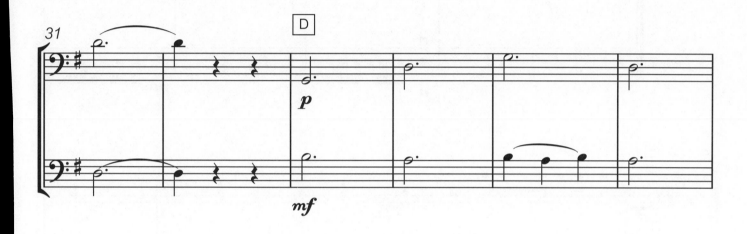

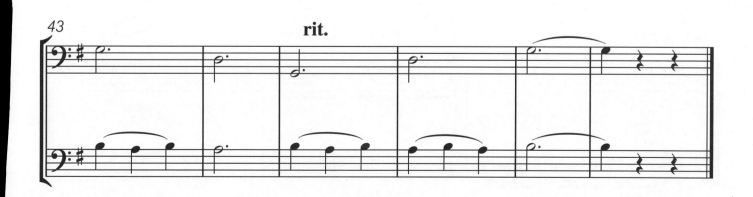

Professor Peg-Box

tries out some dynamic echoes

TECHNICAL TIP: Use more bow for the louder bars and less for the quieter ones
while keeping exactly in time. CHALLENGE: Improvise your own echoes — try
four sets of simple rhythms in 2/4 or 3/4, beginning and ending with a keynote.

Allegro